# The Metaphorest

*poems by*

# Martin Settle

*Finishing Line Press*
Georgetown, Kentucky

# The Metaphorest

*For Brother Peter H. Schmit, my high school biology teacher, who gave me a love for nature that has never died.*

Copyright © 2022 by Martin Settle
ISBN 978-1-64662-908-4 First Edition
All rights reserved under International and Pan-American Copyright Conventions. No part of this book may be reproduced in any manner whatsoever without written permission from the publisher, except in the case of brief quotations embodied in critical articles and reviews.

## ACKNOWLEDGMENTS

"Antidotes." *The Comstock Review*, Spr/Fall 2021
"Birds in Late Autumn." North Carolina Poetry Society. *Pinesong*, Summer 2018
"Bio in Soil," *Kakalak*, 2015, p. 22
"The Great Stream," *Eighth Nazim Hikmet Journal*, 2016, pp. 91-92
"Paper Wasp." *The Comstock Review*, Spring/Summer 2016 30th Anniversary Issue, p. 48
"Remnants." *Pinesong*, 2020, pp. 74-75
"Vibrating the Bee." *The Comstock Review*, Spr/Fall 2017, p.57

Publisher: Leah Huete de Maines
Editor: Christen Kincaid
Cover Art: Martin Settle
Author Photo: John Adams, PhoenixPhotography.us
Cover Design: Elizabeth Maines McCleavy

Order online: www.finishinglinepress.com
also available on amazon.com

Author inquiries and mail orders:
Finishing Line Press
PO Box 1626
Georgetown, Kentucky 40324
USA

# Table of Contents

Antidotes ............................................................................. 1
Pokeweed in the South ................................................... 3
Jewelweed ........................................................................... 4
Poison Hemlock ................................................................. 5
Hunting Morels ................................................................. 7
Giant Puffball .................................................................... 8
Moss ..................................................................................... 9
Kudzu in the Bower ....................................................... 10
Bio in Soil ......................................................................... 11
Oaks .................................................................................... 12
Fireflies ............................................................................. 13
Brief Bio of a Firefly ...................................................... 14
Song of the Water Strider ............................................ 15
Laborare Est Orare ......................................................... 16
Vibrating the Bee ............................................................ 17
Paper Wasp ....................................................................... 18
Moths in the Cosmos .................................................... 19
Shell of the Lettered Olive ........................................... 20
Grunion Run .................................................................... 21
Birds in Late Autumn ................................................... 22
The Eastern Phoebe Returns ....................................... 23
Swarming .......................................................................... 25
The Fox .............................................................................. 26
The Great Stream ........................................................... 28
Attuned with Nature ..................................................... 30
Searching for Peepers .................................................... 32
Remnants .......................................................................... 33
The Metaphorest ............................................................. 35

**Antidotes**

the same plots in life
can hold both poison and antidote
like poison ivy and jewelweed
growing next to one another

soon after my father died
my daughter was born
a coincidence that kept my grief
from blistering over

stinging nettle and dock weed
are another chance pair
that could have soothed my suffering
had I paid attention

my first marriage
was a rash plunge
into the undergrowth
I learned about stinging words
and itching years

after my divorce
poetry healed me
a perennial I hadn't noticed
in disturbed ground
its leaves became a poultice
for my bitterness

identifying the toxic
and its cure is now a habit
I look closely before touching
finding cures in case
of accidental contact

at middle age
vacationing in the Yucatan
I met a young woman
with hair as black as the sap
of the poisonwood tree
she said she loved me
then held out her hand

I took it
knowing it was toxic
we entwined under the shade
of the gumbo limbo tree
its leaves a palliative
that allowed me to rub
away her deceptions
before they set in

I know look-alikes too
no longer fooled by
similarities between Queen Anne's lace
and poison hemlock
or confusing my image in the mirror
with the one in my mind

I have learned anodynes
for the allergies of growing old—
solitude a liniment for loneliness
peace the calamine of passion
creativity a tonic for missing out

death begins to chafe
as my skin has thinned
its red berries beckon
from graves with yew
its seeds have no antidote

**Pokeweed in the South**

in its early stages
pokeweed rises with
hands humble in prayer
as plentiful in spring
as a crop of Christians
at Easter service

then it can be cut
baptized in boiling water
and brought to the table
a poor man's spinach

the ritual can be repeated
the pokeweed does not die
a horizontal tuber
buried in the ground
continues to send up shoots
an immortal that has saved
many from starvation

maturity is the problem
the crimson stems
grow as high as a human
and maiden hair racemes
hang down with purple-black berries
that attract like a woman's nipples

desire comes in seeing the pleasure
of birds feeding
and flying off with berries—
mockingbirds, cardinals, catbirds
eat and sing poke

but humans cannot
even grasp a stalk
without tainting their blood
to eat would be death
the only immortality in these juices
is to write with their ink
or dye with their stain

## Jewelweed

is the woman
who grows by the stream of a young man's bed
he thinks about her before he sleeps
her flowers dangle garish earrings
her lips part into cornucopia

from a distance he hears her laugh at his ardor
she is a cure for a poisonous itch
Touch-Me-Not is her other name
her seed pods swell at the end of summer
he knows they will explode
with the warmth of one finger

## Poison Hemlock

so lush in early spring
along creek banks
like batches of parsley
to garnish a fine meal
surely a sign of good will and utility

first to arise among brittle ruins
the fronds seem to signal
a virtuous work ethic
while others slumber

but do not be deceived
this is appearance only
poison hemlock is a sociopath
deft at making up a story
deadly in its dealings

central to its lying
its imitation of Queen Anne's lace
it grows to the same height
with the same ferny leaves
its umbel spreads out
like a hand offering the same innocence
of the queen's white flowers

yet despite all efforts
to hide murderous intent
it bleeds out in purple spots
along the stem
making it as easy to identify
as the markings of Cain

the enigma of hemlock is
how it hides right out in the open
bold in its malice
without remorse
for the many it has murdered
on its way to the top

Socrates was not fooled
when he drank hemlock
preferring uncompromising truth
to public utterances of ignorance
that had no antidote

## Hunting Morels

you can't be an intellectual
and hunt morels

morels won't be read
won't cultivate
won't respond
to a lens's hot focus

as you walk
morels blend and blur
you must acquire skill
to see subliminally
looking and not looking
for a flicker of sponge
while moving past

but find just one
and you find a village
and you wonder how
you overlooked their huts

to gather morels
you must become feral
a four-legged forest creature
on hands and knees
head nearer the ground

the morel's shape is phallic
turgid in the earth's decay
its musky taste springs
from forbidden realms
below the surface

## Giant Puffball

in a puddle of sunlight
in the forest
it appeared
like an alabaster bust of Homer

I had never seen a mushroom
as large as a human skull
and it seemed to be engaged
in the deepest contemplation

I knew puffballs
and I knew what was inside—
a pure white bread
without gills or guile
edible like manna

to bring this rare find home
would be to feed ten friends
I could hold it up
and say alas poor Yorick
before we consumed it
like an ancient god

to leave it
would be to allow
for the old ways
to survive
it would fill with black spores
and smolder

then to kick it
would raise a smoke
like the beginning of thought

**Moss**

moss covers the low, moist places
pubic hair of forest and stream
it swells in rain
and glistens resurrected
its beauty welcomes nearness
and the brush of a hand

if you want to say
your goodbyes to the dead
moss will outline
the life of a fallen tree
its muted sadness envelops
like velvet in a coffin
its verdure
reverent with silence

never question moss—
where do I go?
moss is an unreliable compass
its tree patches are not blaze marks
moss always tells pilgrims to stay
with generations of monks
wearing down marble steps

bring your desiccation to moss
and view yourself as much smaller
you will not find sustenance for your thirst
but enough to wet your lips
to live on stones

## Kudzu in the Bower

strangler hands are gentle
starting at the feet
they creep gently
up thighs
and whisper

*relax for a season.*
*how far could I go?*

but it isn't long before tendrils
dally around pelvis and breast
with green embrace
and fertile ardor
purple flowers are offered as gifts
scented for romance

in only a few summers
the intimacy of palmate leaves
reaches the throat
and insist upon the deepest kiss
then smothering lips envelop the face
with no resistance from limbs
that give shape to a shroud
breezes speak a last rite
of minister and murderer

*now you know*
*how far I will go*

## A Bio in Soil

the prairie soil of my childhood
was black and glacier blessed
broadcasted seeds
answered in leafy mystery
no neglect was so profuse
that did not fill pockets with chance fruit
or weed so feckless
that could not be made into mother bouquets

as a young man I found an uneven
rock-ridden ground
stones worked to the surface
like doubt
I sowed
but not always reaped
a harsh New England turf
plow shares broken and boulders for fences

middle age was a western desert
deceptive distances and mirages
marriage, a ranch style home
double-car garage
an air that was arid
a soil unquenchable

I have retired
in Carolina soils
furrows are red
with uneasy history
the stunted corn
makes good mash
I am amazed
anything grows at all
in this soil
Adam was fired from

**Oaks**

oaks are to be worshipped
dying and being reborn
through more seasons than
a human memory can hold

their lives can span
a nation's history
recording the years
in their girth
of plenty and drought
lightning strikes and rivers overflowing
amputations and piercings

oak acorns can rain down
like manna
offering salvation in cups
to votaries who know
how to remove bitterness
from a sacrament
they can be cached as alms
to feed the future poor
or left to grow cathedrals

oak branches can stretch out
and still be strong enough
to hold a sacrificial man
or be heavy enough to come crashing down
to cripple a dreamer
they can be made into ax handles
to fell a brother
burned long and evenly
to roast a martyr

oaks are primeval
on winter nights
their shadows flicker on bedroom walls
the terror of ancestral forests
matching the dendrites
of darker regions of the brain

## Fireflies

jars of winking lights
with holes in the lids
were no longer enough
to hold the teen I was

that's when I skewered
the luciferin abdomens
of dozens of fireflies
onto toothpicks

I spelled out her name
in illuminated letters
that shone in the darkness
of my bedroom

when I snuck her into my room
I turned off the lights
so that she could see
the greenish glow of my yearning

I whispered her name
then kissed her
and turned on the lights
but she turned them off again

that memory still flashes
fifty years later
when I first began
to win the fire of a female
by writing with light

**Brief Bio of a Firefly**

I have lain with a woman
sparks rising from a campfire
winking out beneath
the constellations

I have been in the company of males
so frenzied in pursuit of females
that we held up our lanterns
in one encompassing light

I have gone to a monastery
to escape the power
of the genie in the lamp
trying to channel its lightning
into a key

I have been attracted
to the lone woman at the bar
stirring her ice in lunar reflection
and I have alighted next to her cold glow
only to be deceived and devoured

I have been a slave
to the chemistry
of overexcitement and release
my light bent to the momentary
gravity of a body

this has been my life—
flashes of brilliance
that rise only so far
then return to the grasses
small meteoric passages
pretending to be stars

**Song of the Water Strider**

she hears his song
ascending her legs
tickling vibrations
plucked from a harp
of water surface tension

she tries to resist the call
but the player persists
striking the strings
with increasing rhythm

on tiny hairs
she floats
guided by the intensity
kissing at her feet until

suddenly he is there
in the thrum's center
she glides to him
forgetting herself
in more legs
than she has ever known

**Laborare Est Orare**
*to work is to pray— monastic dictum*

in early morning incense
worker bees have found
a magnolia blossom
pure as a Cistercian's sleeve

red-tipped stamens have pooled
at the flower's center
nails from the stigmata
the bees bathe in this pollen cup
until their leg pouches are swollen
then stagger drunken to flight

celibacy is not without its excesses
good news will be greeted in hive
with infinite waggle

I know these bees
as I know white paper
as I know the body in washed linen
as I know shovel and snow
and prayer piled high
believing in the path

### Vibrating the Bee
> *Mere air, these words, but delicious to hear.* —Sappho

breathe in
and you make sugar
breathe out
and your waste is another's dream

breathe in
for bubbles in water
breathe out
for turtles on stone

the leaf on the ground
is a feather
the cat eats
the mockingbird's song

breathe in
for moisture in shadows
breathe out
for prisms in rain

breathe in
to sit next to the fire
breathe out
to nest on the limb

the leaf in the tree
is speaking
the snail in the teeth
is a tongue

breathe in
and your mouth is a flower
breathe out
and you vibrate the bee

**Paper Wasp**

one left
not guarding but surviving
behind the umbrella nest
above my doorway
I doubt he could come up
with a decent sting in December

I'm on a ladder
we look at one another
old males who have served their purpose
the queen has gone to a wood pile
the next generation is launched

this has become a daily routine
checking on him
he seems to know me
moving his antennae in recognition
I take the newspaper inside
doubting he'll last much longer
and I read about the world
I'm no longer a part of

## Moths in the Cosmos

The light departs and moths descend
to beds of cosmos
wings flecked with stars
they feed on dark nectar
such silent work in accident
as they dust anther and pistil heads
pollen falling into flower dreams

much of the inward work of the universe
is done in debris—
gathering galactic arms
secondhand suns reborn in star refuse
black gravity and meteor showers pollinating planets

in sleep tonight I will participate
fluttering eyelids will light up rods and cones
fragments of my days
I have said in sleep I am not asleep
I have heaped shells on vast shores
wondering what work I do while dreaming

## Shell of the Lettered Olive

I wrap myself in solitude
scroll upon scroll
polished to the hardened exterior
writing demands

I do this with persistent
and calculated selfishness
scribbling while streets
are filled with clutching hands
and glaciers melt
creeping up shores

I could share
more intimacies with you
instead I build poems
and offer them to you
leaving dead birds at the door

I do this knowing the impossibility
of ever putting our souls into words
of ever confronting all the whorls
you have been denied because of me
I have tightly wound
my cylinder with a narrow door

for this I know
I deserve to be cast ashore
where sand can wear holes
into my comings and goings
all I ever wanted was to write
what has never been written
I know it's not just
but I'm a happy man in such failure
being so common in your love
as to thrive in shallow waters

## Grunion Run

the moon goddess guides grunion
to shore with silver fingers
no one knows which wave
contains a revelation of fishy flames

standing on their tails
females wriggle holes in sand
deposit eggs for males
to follow with milt
both disappear quickly
dowsed by the next surge

to have them burst at your feet
is to be engulfed in fertility
you want to lie wide-eyed
in an urgency of moisture
shoot seed toward the Milky Way
then ride on a destiny
beyond your breathing

pull is the oldest ritual—
the firmament calls
the deep responds
filling crevices with life
the undertow wants to
take it all back

## Birds of Late Autumn

they look like leaves
the starlings that burst
from the tree leaving it bare

loose threads of geese
blow across the sky
only a hawk remains
circling in a gray caul

my steps crunch magnolia pods
stripped of crimson seeds
by migrating robins

birds that have stayed
finches and sparrows
puff up on wires
doves no longer sing courtship
and a cardinal flits in sere brush
a pilot flame

and me
what kind of reserves
do I have for the coming cold
and a love that just remembers

## The Eastern Phoebe Returns

ah, you're back!
I can see from a distance
your distinctive tail-bob
on our garden fence

and yes
I recognize your surreptitious pause
before you dart under the porch eves—
mustn't be followed

what is it now
five years of calling those rafters
summer home?
you are welcome
in these chaotic times
more than you know
carrying in your beak
moss from the creek bed

you have found
a temporary place of safety
and you build a hopeful nest
next to the previous four
we have a trusting relationship
I have heard your chicks' cheep
unafraid as I passed beneath

only once have I violated
our non-interference pact
taking out a ladder
and looking in on your nursery
three mouths larger than their bodies
greeted in hungry expectation
if anything happened to you
I would feed them

I am getting old
and it seems that delight
comes to me most often

as return
you reassure me
that old weather cycles
and migratory patterns will hold
at least until I die

**Swarming**

I do not know what keeps
these birds together and apart
or why they are chained and free

over cornfield stubble
hundreds of starlings
twist and turn
a tattered scarf in the wind

their wings flash out silver
when they angle into the sun
then darken in density
as they gather to land

suddenly all rise again
by some unseen signal
to disappear into the distance
a dust storm on the horizon

in the void of their departure
I long for the beauty of such synchrony
even speaking the same language
with my neighbor
we never mesh
right and left
up and down

## The Fox

I conjured you
in the forest
sitting against a tree

the guidebook I read
had words that
wanted to be world

when I looked up
you were there
sitting on haunches

your pointed nose swayed
like a conductor's baton
to the birds flitting in trees

you did not see me
but I saw with intimacy
your raw curiosity

no creature as canny as you
can live without time
to be beguiled

then you continued
trotting carelessly
almost into my lap

shocked
we both froze
at such proximity

our eyes held
burning a rent
between civil and wild

in seconds I found
more to imagine
than I could ever sustain

when I blinked
your tail disappeared
closing a seam in the brush

**The Great Stream**
*in remembrance of Don Chamberlain (1952-2014)*

testing the waters
I find nymphs beneath the stones
trout, you said,
only exist in the purest streams

fog rises in patches from deeper pools
there are ghosts this morning
signs radiate beneath the watery mirror
where mouths feed on the surface

I see the short-lived caddis flies
swarming in filtered light
a new hatch urgent to mate
they will be today's communion

I choose the sympathetic fly—
*match the hatch* you said—
and I tie the knot you taught me
seven ritualistic loops tightened with spit
to secure the hook

I cannot fish without your presence
the signs were there for you too
polluting poisons from the pancreas
that bloated your abdomen
and darkened your urine
the doctors told you
your time would be brief

then we fished and fished
laying out line after line
casting in companionship to catch hope
in the end you could barely walk the water
but you continued
until your colon silted up in cancerous sand

I walk up midstream alone now
fishing like we used to
my line laying out offerings

like a magician's hand
a large trout rises from the pool
I feel the tug, then taut fight for life
innocence fooled to the death
soon it will be part of me

you never believed in god
I can only say I believe the great stream
that moves through the Milky Way
is speckled with life
carrying with it mysteries
of eat and eaten and return
it would not surprise me in this flow
to see you up ahead

**Attuned with Nature**

attuned means never buying flowers
means giving flowers you can eat
attuned is never going hungry
always confident touching
finding sculptures on the ground
keeping an eye out and an eye in

morels are a feast day
on the calendar
I search knowing I will find
they are there every year
same time   same place
I gather the spongy currency
with little investment

attuned is recognition
shifts foreground and background
carries a knife to harvest
has no category called weed
attuned is effortless
knowledgeable not lucky
knowing the seasons to look up
the seasons to look down

the log across my pathway
is not an obstacle
but an offering of oyster mushrooms
I gather dinner as I climb over
then go on my way
a new menu percolating
in my mind for the evening meal
finding without seeking

attuned means knowing the times
of the shad and shadberry
the appearance of the mountain's blue ghosts
means never being able
to turn a complete circle
without being interrupted
by truth and beauty

attuned is spontaneity earned
mixes seeking and finding
puts an ear to the sugar maple
to hear the sap rising

**Searching for Peepers**

I cannot find the source
of that sound
thumb on a comb

I have come to open fields
bending down to pull up hands
filled with nothing but mud

maybe it's my shadow
maybe gravity gives me away

when I withdraw far enough
where nothing can be captured
this sluice begins churning again

I must learn this amphibian trick
to sing and disappear

**Remnants**
> *Thinking is polytheistic.*    —Paul Shepard

### 1
monadnock
in Stone Mountain State Park
a partially buried skull
with nimbus of vultures
climbers go up a fissure
like scientists with tape measures

### 2
visitor center displays
a mounted black bear
old saint of religions
of caves and rebirth
homesteading tools cover walls
artifacts of early conquest

### 3
at the trailhead a coke machine
begs offerings from pilgrims
I climb in silence
through oak-hickory forests
blaze-marked trails
make it difficult to forget
human presence

### 4
a scent draws me from the path
into a moss-covered ravine
she is there before an overhang
goddess in white cymes
backlit by a filtered sun
her name is not in my tree guide

### 5
I am lost
gratefully for awhile
making my own path up
to the summit
smooth igneous rock is pocked

with islands of pine
I take off my socks and shoes
for a closer grip

6
in humility of no roads
the view is almost virginal
I imagine wilderness without end
filled with numinous nooks
I want to build a cairn
but among the rocks a soda can
new god that is ubiquitous

7
when the park closes
the sun sets with colors
of a polluting presence
the moon rises
and a cult of remnant creatures
come out of sacred groves
they worship in the ancient ways
beneath a haloed moon
the moon that was a god
before the boot prints of monotheism

## The Metaphorest
> *No ideas but in things*       —W.C. Williams

is an ancient forest
with trees whose girths
are as old as language
whose roots
drink from a soil
of syntax and grammar

all the species in these woods
have become words—
to kill anything
would be to lose vocabulary

there is hopping, slithering, climbing,
flying, walking, swimming, burrowing
one is in the midst of choreographed purposes
nodding, rooting, flowering,
pollinating, budding, fruiting,
one is in the midst of synthesis

once I tried to write
without the metaphorest
but pubic hair was not mossy
fireflies could not light up desire
kudzu was not a strangling murderer
love did not reside on lettered olive shells
nor celibate Cistercians become bees

my poems could not escape
an animal from creeping in
or a seed from taking root
I could not speak apart
from taxonomy
a hunt that guided my words
to waterholes
where creation drank

in the metaphorest
you must wear a mask
there is no such thing as *you*
without the others

I have been the fox
to know cunning
and the compass plant
to meditate on the sun
I have flecked my face
like a moth wing to enter the cosmos
mottled my skin to disappear
like a peeper frog

my desire to write
has deepened
I long to be a symbiotic fungus
living among roots
an organism that feeds
while it connects living things
I wear the mask
of this small role
without it
I know only loneliness

www.ingramcontent.com/pod-product-compliance
Lightning Source LLC
LaVergne TN
LVHW041558070426
835507LV00011B/1156